Dealing With Waste

HOUSEHOLD WASTE

Sally Morgan

A+
Smart Apple Media

This book has been published in cooperation with Franklin Watts.

Editor: Rachel Minay, Designer: Brenda Cole, Picture research: Morgan Interactive Ltd., Consultant: Graham Williams

Picture credits:
The publishers would like to thank the following for reproducing these photographs:
Digitalvision front cover main image & top right; Ecoscene front cover bottom right (Angela Hampton), 6 (Jon Bower), 7 (Rod Gill), 8 (Alan Towse), 9 (Sally Morgan), 10 (Tom Ennis), 11 (Luc Hosten), 12 (Nick Hawkes), 13 (Vicki Coombs), 14 (Adrian Morgan), 15 (Lorenzo Lees), 16 (Vicki Coombs), 17 (Angela Hampton), 18 (Alan Towse), 19 (Nick Hanna), 21 (Phillip Colla), 22 (Vicki Coombs), 23 (Wayne Lawler), 24 (Martin Jones), 25 (Latha Raman), 26 (Peter Landon), 27 (Angela Hampton).

Published in the United States by Smart Apple Media
2140 Howard Drive West, North Mankato, Minnesota 56003

Library of Congress Cataloging-in-Publication Data

Morgan, Sally.
Household waste / by Sally Morgan.
p. cm. – (Dealing with waste)
Includes index.
ISBN-13: 978-1-59920-008-8
[1. Refuse and refuse disposal.] I. Title.

TD791.M73 2007
363.72'88–dc22   2006035135

9 8 7 6 5 4 3 2 1

Contents

Mountains of waste

Every day we throw away mountains of waste. This includes packaging from food and goods, paper and envelopes, cans and bottles, plastic bags, kitchen waste, and much more.

Shoppers crowd this street in Shenyang, China. As the standard of living increases in countries such as China, the waste problem will grow.

More people, more waste

As the number of people in the world increases, so does the amount of waste. However, not all parts of the world produce the same amount of waste. A typical home in a developed country such as the United States, United Kingdom (UK), or Germany produces many times more waste than a home in a developing country such as Kenya, Ghana, or India. For example, on average, a person in the U.S. produces about 5.5 lbs (2 kg) of waste per day, a person in Europe produces about 2.4 lbs (1.1 kg) per day, while a person living in India produces just over 1.1 lb (0.5 kg) of waste per day.

Thrown away

As people earn more money, they buy more goods, especially electrical goods and luxury items. They throw away more, too. The world is changing from one where people repaired broken goods or reused them to one in which broken objects are tossed away and replaced by new ones. The manufacturing of all of these goods is using up the world's resources.

In some places, waste is dumped on the side of the road, creating an unsightly mess and attracting pests such as rats and mice.

It's my world!

How much waste does your family produce each day? Put one day's waste into a bag and weigh it. Can you work out how much your family would throw away in a year?

Harming the environment

Waste can be very harmful to the environment if it is not disposed of carefully. Also, the increasing volumes of waste create problems for the people who have to dispose of it. The world cannot continue to create so much waste—everybody will have to find ways of reducing it.

In this book, you will read about the different types of waste that people produce and how we deal with it.

What's in your garbage?

People throw away many kinds of things. Much of the waste comes from the kitchen or garden. There are food scraps, lawn clippings, and weeds as well as paper, plastic, and metals.

Biodegradable waste

Food and garden waste is described as being biodegradable. This means that it will rot or break down naturally. The first stages of this rotting process often take place in the garbage can when food goes moldy and becomes smelly! Some people put a lot of garden waste in their garbage can. This type of waste should be put on a compost heap where microorganisms such as bacteria and fungi break it down.

Compost needs a good mix of materials such as food scraps and grass clippings to make sure it does not turn into a sloppy mess. Shredded paper and cardboard can also be composted.

It's my world!

Not everybody has a compost pile. However, many towns and cities have facilities where people can take their garden waste. The waste is put on large compost heaps where it breaks down to form compost, which people can buy to put on their gardens. Find out where your local compost facilities are located. This information can often be found on the Internet.

Other waste

A lot of paper is thrown away, too. This includes newspapers, magazines, old envelopes, junk mail, paper, and cardboard boxes. There is also paper packaging from food and household goods. The rest of the waste is made of plastic, metals, and glass, together with old clothes, unwanted toys, other household items, and things that have been broken beyond repair.

paper 25%

kitchen and garden waste 35%

metal 9%

plastic 11%

other items 11%

glass 9%

Much of this garbage could have been recycled, including all of the glass and metal and most of the plastic and paper. All of the kitchen and garden waste could have been composted. That adds up to about 80% of the waste.

Dangerous waste

Some of the things that we throw away can harm the environment. For example, old batteries contain metals that are poisonous to wildlife. Sometimes people throw away unused medicines, which should be returned to the pharmacy to be disposed of properly. Many chemicals are used in the garden, which should not be put in the garbage but disposed of carefully.

Where does your waste go?

What happens to the waste you throw out? In most developed countries, the waste is collected and taken to either landfill sites or incinerators. However, in much of the developing world, garbage is just dumped in the countryside.

Landfills

Landfills are huge holes in the ground, often left by gravel pits and quarries. The hole is gradually filled with waste from homes and industry. Each day, tractors squash the waste down so that it is all compacted together with no holes. Once the hole is full, the top is covered with a layer of soil. After about 10 years, the land can be used for farming or as a park.

Dumping waste in a hole is easy, but landfills cause problems. People do not like living near them because the waste attracts pests such as rats and seagulls. Landfills can be smelly places. As all the food and garden waste rots down, it releases a gas called methane. This gas has to be piped away—otherwise it could cause an explosion. Also, there are only a limited number of landfills and they are rapidly filling up.

This bulldozer is moving and flattening the waste that has been dumped in a landfill. The food in the waste attracts flocks of gulls.

It's my world!

Never litter the environment because it can harm animals. Animals may crawl into bottles and cans looking for food and become trapped. Birds may become entangled in plastic netting or get their necks trapped in plastic rings. Broken glass on the ground could cut the feet of people as well as animals.

Incinerators

Incinerators are places where waste is burned. Some modern incinerators use the heat produced by the burning waste to generate electricity. These incinerators are called waste-to-energy plants. There are problems with incinerators, though. The smoke from incinerators may contain dangerous chemicals such as dioxin. Tiny quantities of this chemical can cause ill health or even kill people.

Better to recycle

Much of the waste that ends up in landfills and incinerators could be recycled. If it is recycled, it can be used to make something else. This is much better for the environment.

This gannet on a beach in South Africa has become entangled in a sheet of plastic. Many animals die each year after becoming tangled in plastic.

Reduce, reuse, and recycle

The three "R's" of managing waste are "reduce," "reuse," and "recycle." Reduce means to cut down on the amount of waste, reuse means to put something to a new use or to fix it rather than throw it away, and recycle means to make a material into a new product.

Fruit and vegetables in a market are sold without unnecessary packaging. In the supermarket, you can choose loose rather than prepackaged produce.

Reduce and reuse

It is much better to not produce any waste in the first place. If less waste is thrown away, there is less waste to bury in landfills or burn in incinerators. For example, disposable diapers are a substantial part of household waste in houses where there is a baby. This could be avoided by using washable diapers. The next best way to deal with waste is to reuse it. For example, old plastic pots can be used as plant pots. Another way of reusing something is to sell it or give it to a charity shop or yard sale. If something cannot be reused, then the next best thing is to recycle it.

It's my world!

Try to reduce the amount of packaging in your waste. Always take a shopping bag with you so you don't have to pick up lots of new plastic bags. Try to choose goods with fewer layers of unnecessary packaging. Once you have removed all the packaging, make sure you recycle as much of it as possible.

Recycle

Recycling means to make something into a new item—for example, a glass bottle can be melted and made into a new bottle, while old cardboard can be shredded and made into new cardboard. Virtually all of the world's countries have recycling programs. A wide range of items can be recycled, but the most common are glass, paper, metal, plastic, old clothes, oil, and batteries. There are recycling facilities such as aluminum and plastic recycling bins near stores and parking lots, and items for recycling are often collected from the home.

So remember the three "R's"—reduce, reuse, and recycle. It is always better to reduce first, then to reuse, and finally to recycle something.

Yard sales are good places to sell unwanted toys, books, clothes, and other household goods.

Dealing with glass

Glass is a very useful material. It can be made into bottles, jars, and other containers to hold liquids and foods. Also, it can be recycled over and over again.

Reusing glass bottles

It is much better for the environment's sake to reuse a glass bottle than to recycle it. Glass bottles can be collected, washed, and refilled. Bottles that are reused need to be a bit heavier than other bottles so that they do not break or chip easily. Some glass bottles may be reused more than 30 times and have a life of four years. In the developing world, it is common for glass bottles to be collected and reused.

These glass bottles outside a shop in Jakarta, Indonesia, are awaiting collection. They will be taken to the local factory, cleaned, and refilled.

Recycling glass bottles

Bottles to be recycled are collected at recycling centers. The glass is crushed to form cullet, which is transported to glass factories.

Glass is made from sand, soda ash, and limestone. Additives may be used to give the glass a color or to make it more resistant to heat. These raw materials are heated in a furnace to 3,272°F (1,800°C) so they melt. The molten glass is poured into molds to form new bottles. Cullet is usually added to the furnace with the raw materials, so fewer raw materials are required to make the glass.

Clear glass is the most valuable because it has many uses. A lot of brown glass is used for beer bottles. Green glass is the least useful and is used mostly for wine bottles. Glass also can be recycled to make garden paving, decorative jewelry, and a road surface called glasphalt.

The different colored glass has to be kept separate, so there are usually three bins—one each for clear, green, and brown glass.

Make sure that every glass bottle and container used by your family is recycled. There are plenty of glass-recycling centers. Local authorities have recycling facilities that will accept glass. In some places, glass is collected from homes.

Benefits of recycling

Recycling glass saves energy because glass made with cullet melts at a lower temperature than glass made from raw materials, so less energy is used to heat the materials in the furnace. It reduces the air pollution produced by glass manufacturing by 20 percent and the water pollution by 50 percent. It means less glass ends up in landfills and less broken glass is lying around to harm people and wildlife.

Paper and cardboard

Paper is an incredibly useful material that is used in newspapers, magazines, and books. One of its most common uses is in packaging for food and other goods. Some paper, such as newspaper, is already made from recycled paper. Most other paper can also be recycled after use.

This waste paper has been sorted and baled. Recycling paper reduces the amount of waste that ends up in landfill sites.

From paper bank to paper mill

Paper to be recycled must be sorted, graded, and baled before it can be transported to a paper mill. In the paper mill, the recycled paper is broken up into a pulp. It is then mixed with lots of water and chemicals to make a mush that is used to form paper. Sometimes, some unrecycled pulp is added to improve the quality of the final paper. The runny mush is spread out over a moving belt of the paper machine, and the water drains away. The paper is now a continuous layer and is passed through a series of heated rollers so that it is flattened, dried, and ironed to give it a polished surface. Finally the paper is rolled onto huge reels and taken to the cutting room to be cut into sheets.

Fibers

If you look at paper under a microscope, you will see that it is made from lots of fibers squashed together. The longer the fiber is, the better quality the paper. However, each time paper is recycled, the fibers get shorter. Shorter lengths of fiber make poorer quality paper such as newspaper print. One of the biggest users of recycled paper is the newspaper industry. Other poor quality paper is recycled to make cardboard and toilet paper.

When you buy stationery in a store, check the packaging to see if it has been made from recycled paper.

It's my world!

There are many ways to reduce the use of paper.

▶ Scraps of paper can be made into notebooks.

▶ Throw away a sheet of paper only if it has been written on both sides.

▶ Don't print out unnecessary pages on your printer—look at them on the screen instead.

▶ E-mails are quicker and cheaper to send than a letter, and they don't use any paper or envelopes.

▶ Reuse envelopes by sticking a label over the old address.

Other uses of paper

Not all paper is recycled back to paper. Now it is possible to buy animal bedding that is made from recycled paper. Paper can also be made into a "fluff" that is used to insulate homes. The fluff is pumped into the gap between the inner and outer walls to prevent heat from escaping. Some recycled paper is also used to make disposable diapers.

Metals for recycling

Metals are valuable materials because they can be used in many ways. A variety of metals can be found in the home: steel and aluminum in cans and aerosols, lead on the roof, copper on the pipes, and gold and silver in jewelry.

Metal cans are moved along a conveyor belt in a large recycling center in Florida. They will be crushed, baled, and sent to a factory, where they will be melted down.

Where metal comes from

Most metals cannot be dug straight from the ground. A metal usually occurs as an ore; for example, iron is found in iron ore and aluminum occurs as an ore called bauxite. The ores are found in rocks that have to be quarried or mined from the ground. Then the ores have to be crushed and transported to factories, where they are heated to high temperatures to extract the metal.

Easy to recycle

Recycling metal is much easier compared with extracting the metal from rocks. Metals are very easy to recycle, and they can be recycled over and over again. Waste metal is tipped into a large furnace and heated to a high temperature so that it melts. The molten metal is poured into a mold to make an ingot. The ingots are stored until the metal is needed to make something. Then it is melted again and reshaped into a new object.

Helping the environment

Recycling metal helps the environment. A lot of fuel is used to remove the rocks from the ground and then transport them around the world. More fuel is needed to extract the metal from the rock. In comparison, melting down old metal takes much less energy. The extraction process creates air and water pollution, too. Mining and quarrying damage habitats. Often, quarries are located in attractive parts of the countryside, and they create unsightly scars. Recycling metal takes place locally, so the metal does not need to be transported far.

Did you know . . .

Steel and aluminum cans look very similar. One way to tell them apart is to use a magnet. Steel is magnetic, so a steel can will stick to a magnet. Aluminum is not magnetic, so a magnet will not pick up an aluminum can. It is important to be able to tell the difference because the two metals must be kept separate when they are recycled. Test some cans yourself to see if they are magnetic or not. You may need to check the top and the sides of the can because the sides and ends are sometimes made from different metals.

Quarries, such as this bauxite quarry in Jamaica, destroy habitats and create piles of waste. The quarried rock is crushed and shipped overseas.

Recycling plastics

Plastics are useful materials. Each year, 110 million tons (100 million t) of plastics are made around the world. That uses up a lot of oil.

What is plastic?

Most plastics are made from oil. Plastics are made of long chains of molecules that are formed when oil is heated. There are more than 50 different groups of plastic. Hard plastics are used to make containers and bottles. Thin and flexible plastics are used to make plastic bags. Foam-like plastics are used in disposable plastic cups and takeout containers. All of these different plastics must be kept separate when they are recycled.

Identifying plastics

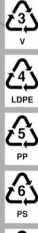

	Polyethylene terephthalate	Drink bottles and oven-ready meal trays
	High-density polyethylene	Bottles for milk and cleaning liquids
	Polyvinyl chloride	Food trays, plastic wrap, soda pop bottles, and shampoo bottles
	Low density polyethylene	Grocery bags and garbage bags
	Polypropylene	Margarine tubs, microwaveable meal trays
	Polystyrene	Foam food trays, egg cartons, foam cups, plastic cutlery
		Any other plastics that do not fall into the above categories such as melamine, which is used in plastic plates and cups

Sorting plastic

It is possible to recycle almost all kinds of plastic, but only a few types are recycled at the moment. This is because some plastics, such as blended plastics (which are made from several types of plastic), are very difficult to recycle. Recycling certain plastics can damage the environment because they release harmful chemicals during the recycling process, so it is better not to recycle them. Plastic bottles are the most useful, while plastic food wrappers are not widely recycled. To make it easier for the public and the people who sort plastics at recycling centers, most plastic items carry a logo (see table), which identifies the type of plastic from which they are made. The logo is a recycling triangle with a number in the middle—the number identifies the plastic.

It's my world!

How many plastic bags did you pick up from stores this week? Try to reduce the number of plastic bags you need by using strong reusable bags for your shopping. You can reuse plastic bags to line garbage cans. Plastic containers can be useful, too. Try using them as pots for planting or as containers for small objects such as buttons, nails, and screws. Attractive containers can be used on a desk for paper clips and pens.

Processing plastic

Before plastic waste can be recycled, it must be separated into different types and colors. Then it is cleaned, shredded into small flakes, and bagged. The flakes are transported to factories, where they are heated so that they melt and are shaped into new objects. A wide range of items can be made from recycled plastic, for example, garbage bags, plant pots, drain pipes, animal feed troughs, window frames, fencing, and garden benches and chairs. Plastic bottles are even made into fleece clothes.

These tourists watching the Old Faithful Geyser in Yellowstone National Park are standing on a viewing platform made from recycled plastic.

Dangerous waste

People throw many things into the garbage without thinking about whether they are safe. A number of dangerous chemicals are used in the home, and if they get into the environment, they can harm wildlife.

Chemicals in the garden shed

Many harmful chemicals may be found in the garden shed or garage. These include pesticides, weed killers, and slug pellets. There may be cans of old paint, paint thinner, or antifreeze. All of these chemicals could harm the environment if they were washed down the drain, leaked out of the garbage, or were dumped in a landfill.

Chemicals for cleaning

The cupboard under the kitchen sink is often packed with cleaning materials such as bleach and other chemicals. Some are so powerful that the person using them must wear protective gloves. Such contents should never be dumped down the sink or put in the garbage without being securely wrapped to prevent leaks.

Paint contains harmful chemicals. Leftover paint should never be dumped down the drain or sink. There is usually somewhere in your local area where paint can be disposed of safely.

Harmful batteries

Batteries contain metals such as mercury, nickel, and cadmium, all of which are very harmful. Single-use batteries, or alkaline batteries, are thrown away once they are flat. They contain metals such as mercury, silver, or zinc. Rechargeable batteries or nicads contain the metals nickel and cadmium, which are also hazardous. Lithium ion batteries are used in laptops, but they are not considered to be dangerous. The amount of harmful metal used in batteries, has been declining in recent years, and now it is possible to buy mercury-free batteries. Often, there are collection points for old batteries in stores and at recycling centers.

When chemical containers, even empty ones, are dumped into landfill sites, there is a possibility that any liquid in the container will drain into the soil.

Did you know . . .

There are many potentially harmful chemicals in the home. Some of the most common ones are:

- ▶ bleach
- ▶ oven cleaner
- ▶ solvents in glue and cleaning agents
- ▶ paint thinner
- ▶ pesticide
- ▶ weed killer
- ▶ slug pellets
- ▶ batteries
- ▶ antifreeze
- ▶ unwanted or outdated medicines
- ▶ fluorescent light bulbs

It's my world!

The chemicals mentioned on this page have to be disposed of carefully so that they do not harm the environment. Local authorities usually have Web sites telling you where to take different chemicals and how to wrap them up.

The developing world

There is far less waste in the developing world. People cannot afford to throw things away, so there is much more reuse and recycling of unwanted items.

These oil cans have been made from old beer cans.

Waste scavengers

There are huge waste dumps in some cities of the developing world such as Mexico City, Mexico, and Manila in the Philippines. People spend their days searching through the waste for useful items. These people are called waste scavengers, and they earn their living by collecting and selling waste. They are often women and children, and they work with little protection for their hands and feet. However, waste scavengers have an important role to play. They make sure that all the recyclable materials are removed and recycled. This reduces the amount of waste that is in the dump.

Making new from old

Many things are never thrown away but are reused to make new items; for example, rubber soles are removed from old shoes and stuck onto new ones, while aluminum cans are used as building materials. Toys can be made from old wheels and pieces of wire. By being creative, people can make a wide range of essential items from waste.

It's my world!

Imagine that you had to find a present for a friend, but you didn't have any money. Could you make something from recycled items such as old wheels, metal coat hangers, string, pieces of wood, and plastic?

Plastic garbage

Lots of plastic bags are used around the world. Unfortunately, in some developing countries, garbage is left on the streets; the plastic bags blow away in the wind and litter the streets. Plastic litter is a big problem in some countries such as The Gambia. The bags get caught on fences and trees or end up in rivers. Sometimes animals get caught in the plastic bags and they can die. Countries such as South Africa and Bangladesh are now banning the manufacture of plastic bags.

Did you know . . .

India recycles about 60 percent of the plastic used each year, a figure higher than any other country. The average for the rest of the world is about 20 percent. India is able to achieve such a high rate because wages are low and recycling companies can afford to employ the many people needed to sort through all the plastic waste.

These Indian workers are sorting different types of plastic. The plastic could cut their skin or be covered in harmful substances, but they do not wear any protective clothing or gloves on their hands.

The way ahead

The amount of waste that is being produced by people is increasing every year. Landfill sites are filling up and it has become more expensive to dispose of all the waste. Somehow, more waste will have to be recycled.

Goods such as Easter eggs and boxes of chocolates come with layers of unnecessary packaging.

Encouraging recycling

One way to encourage people to throw away less is to charge them for every pound of waste they put out for collection. In the U.S., this is called "Pay-As-You-Throw," and it has resulted in a sharp decrease in the amount of waste. Often, people are more likely to recycle if the items are collected from their own homes rather than if they have to drive to a recycling center.

Passing laws

Governments can encourage more recycling by making manufacturers responsible for disposing of items such as packaging. Laws can be passed that require manufacturers to use a certain percentage of recycled materials in their manufacturing processes.

If your home does not have recycling collection, simply place all of the bottles and other items that can be recycled in a box, and when you go shopping with your family, they can be emptied into recycling bins.

Creating a demand

Recycling centers need a market for recycled materials. There is no point in collecting glass or plastic for recycling if nobody wants to buy it. So, it is important that people buy items containing recycled materials. This will create a demand for the recycled materials, and they will become more valuable. When a recycled material is valuable, such as metal, people are more likely to want to recycle it.

When you buy stationery, such as notepads or envelopes, check to see if it is made from recycled paper. If it is, it will have a recycling logo with a percentage in the middle. This tells you exactly how much recycled paper was used in its manufacturing.

It's my world!

There are many ways to reduce the amount of garbage you and your family throw away each week. See if you can cut down on your waste. Some ways are very simple. Recycle as much as possible by not putting glass, paper, plastic, or metal in the garbage can. See what else you could recycle—for example, batteries and old clothes. If you have a garden, put food scraps on a compost heap, or see if your area has a food composting center.

Glossary

Biodegradable
able to be broken down naturally by microorganisms such as bacteria and fungi

Compost
to break down waste garden matter; compost is a soil-like material that is full of nutrients

Cullet
broken or waste glass to be recycled

Developed country
a country in which most people have a high standard of living

Developing country
a country in which most people have a low standard of living and poor access to goods and services compared with people in a developed country

Incinerator
a place where waste is burned

Ingot
a block of metal such as gold, silver, or steel

Landfill
a large hole in the ground that is used to dispose of waste

Ore
a type of rock that contains metal in large enough quantities to be mined

Pollution
the release of harmful substances into the environment

Recycle
to process and reuse materials in order to make new items

Reduce
to lower the amount of waste that is produced

Reuse
to use something again, either in the same way or in a different way

Waste
anything that is thrown away, abandoned, or released into the environment in a way that could harm the environment

Web sites

British Glass Recycling
www.recyclingglass.co.uk
Web site about recycling glass in the UK, aimed primarily at young people.

Can Smart
www.cansmart.org
Australian Web site dealing with the recycling of steel cans.

Earth 911
www.earth911.org/master.asp
This Web site shows a variety of national and local U.S. recycling programs and events.

Freecycle
www.freecycle.com
Web site where members can send e-mails to other members of the group listing items that they want to recycle free of charge rather than dumping on a landfill site.

Household Waste
www.purdue.edu/dp/envirosoft/
housewaste/src/open.htm
Learn about the Household Ecosystem at this educational Web site.

Kids' Stuff Recycling
www.deq.state.ms.us/MEDQ.nsf/page/
Recycling_kidsStuff?OpenDocument
Learn more about reducing household waste.

Let's Recycle
www.letsrecycle.com/index.jsp
Web site looking at all sorts of waste and how it can be recycled.

United States Environmental Protection Agency
www.epa.gov
This Web site has lots of environmental information on all issues, not just waste. There is an EPA Kids Club (www.epa.gov/kids) with information on waste and recycling.

U.S. Recycling
www.usrecycleink.com
At this Web site, learn about recycling fundraisers.

World Aluminum Institute
www.world-aluminium.org
Web site with details about aluminum: where it is found, and how it is extracted, then recycled.

Index